Lecce Italy Travel Tips

Discover the most up-to-date and amazing
places to sleep, eat, and shop in the Apulia
region (Lecce), along with essential information
about the city

Hudson Miles

Table Of Contents

Visa

If you are not a citizen of a European Union (EU) or Schengen Area nation, you will usually need a visa to enter Italy. The reason and duration of your stay may necessitate a different visa.

Requirements may vary based on the type of visa (tourist, work, study, etc.). Generally, you'll need a completed application form, passport, passport-sized photos, travel itinerary, proof of accommodation, financial means, and, depending on the visa type, additional documents

Click on the link or scan the QR code.
https://vistoperitalia.esteri.it/home/en

You can also download the visa application form, fill it out, print it, and bring it to the Visa Application Centre for submission.
Refer to the details of the Tourist Office in this guide for additional personal information.

Lecce

95,000 people live in Lecce, which is the biggest city in Puglia's southern region. It is most likely the primary tourist destination in the area and in the southern portion of Italy's mainland. Although erroneous, the term "the Florence of the South" does no honour to the place. The concentration of baroque, primarily ecclesiastical, structures in Lecce's heart is the outcome of the city's explosive growth in the 17th century, a time of great prosperity.

The Messapii established the city in pre-Roman times, and there have been close cultural ties with Greece ever since. After the Ostrogoths destroyed the city in the years after the Roman Empire fell, the Byzantines, Saracens, Lombards, Hungarians, and Slavs briefly controlled it until the Norman invasion in the eleventh century, at which point it became a significant region of the Kingdom of Sicily.

Following the Holy League's (an alliance of Catholic maritime kingdoms) victory against Ottoman forces at the pivotal naval Battle of Lepanto in 1572, there was a comparatively abrupt growth in the 17th century.

As a result, the Salento and its capital city Lecce were freed from the ongoing threat of Turkish invasions and assaults, enabling them to take advantage of the area's abundant agricultural resources and strategic location for trade.
Institutions from the civic, business, and religious sectors particularly fought to flaunt their riches and influence. The appealing pale orange/yellow limestone from the area is weather resistant and simple to carve.

Therefore, Lecce is the best place to go if ornately decorated buildings appeal to you; nowhere else in the world will you find a more densely packed display of saints, flowers, small lads (putti), dragons, etc. It's intriguing to consider that much of the Lecce Centre was built during the era of Samuel Pepys, the Great Fire of London, and the English Civil War.

The **Duomo and Piazza Sant'Oronzo**, which are connected by Via Vittorio Emanuele, form the centre of mediaeval Lecce. About 20 notable baroque churches may be found within a short stroll of Piazza Sant'Oronzo; we highlight a few of them here, with Santa Croce being the finest example of Italian baroque church architecture. Piazza Sant'Oronzo is home to the Castello as well as several other noteworthy Roman locations.

There are plenty of parking alternatives outside the downtown area if you are driving to Lecce. From all throughout Puglia, Lecce is conveniently accessible by train. Direct trains depart from Foggia, Bari, Ostuni, and Brindisi.

For long-distance trains from Rome, Turin, Venice, Milan, and Bologna, this is the "end of the queue". If you arrive by train, simply walk straight out of the station along the Viale Oronzo Quarta, which is bordered with trees. After a few minutes, you will reach the Duomo and Via Vittorio Emanuele by continuing straight and crossing a major road.

Duomo Square
This is a sizable open area that is nearly completely encircled by the Duomo and other nearby religious structures. The Piazza's main entrance is on Via Vittorio Emanuele, which is unexpectedly narrow and conceals this significant public area from the surrounding business district. Overlooking the Piazza is a 55-metre-tall Campanile.

The Cattedrale di Lecce, also known as the Duomo, was established in 1145 and rebuilt in 1229, possibly as a result of foundation issues. It is dedicated to Maria Santissima Assunta. The cathedral began to have structural issues in the late 16th century, and the elaborate exterior and interior design of the structure were substantially shaped during the next 100 years.

Every structure in Piazza Duomo is exquisitely decorated and intended to astonish. The sturdy and commanding Palazzo del Seminario is the most striking. Built between 1695 and 1708, with an additional attic floor erected in 1628.

This structure now contains a number of offices, archives, and a significant library related to the Lecce

Diocese. The Diocesan Museum is also located there. This includes artwork that depicts Lecce's religious life and history, as well as sculptures, silverware and liturgical garments.

The museum costs 5 euros and is accessible Monday through Saturday from 9.0 to 12.30. It's worth spending a euro to enter the cloisters if you're not interested in seeing the museum itself.

By way of Vittorio Emanuele

This is a pedestrian-only area with tons of eateries, bakeries, and bars along with excellent shopping possibilities. Papier-mache figurines are a traditional artistic element of Lecce, and several stores specialise in them.

The municipal and economic hub of Lecce, Piazza Sant'Oronzo, is connected to the Piazza Duomo via Via Vittorio Emanuele. Particularly in the nights, the street is quite bustling. People will come up to you and offer you samples of the cakes and pastries that Lecce is so well known for.

Sant'Oronzo Square

Despite being the "heart" of Lecce, this piazza is not very appealing due to the massive structures from the 20th century that dominate it and the excessive number of cars that are parked or in motion.

The best of various information stations in Lecce, most of which are little more than private travel companies, is a new information centre where you can pick up pamphlets and other materials.

The 28-meter-tall Colonna (Column) in the centre of the Piazza is topped by a 5-metre-tall Statue of Sant'Oronzo, the first Bishop of Lecce in the fourth century. The column itself is Roman in origin; it was given to Lecce by the City of Brindisi in 1680 and is the twin of the column that marks the end of the Appian Way in Brindisi.

At this point, Sant'Oronzo was declared the patron saint of both Ostuni and Lecce, and it is said that he prevented the plague from striking both cities. The marble column was in ruins on the ground in "drums" in Brindisi at the time.

The mayor of Brindisi at the time was inspired to give it to Lecce, but the city's residents fiercely opposed it.

Since then, there have been multiple attempts—some of which are ongoing—to have it restored and erected in its original location.

The statue, a hollow wooden frame plated in bronze, was created in Venice in 1794 to replace an earlier one that had been damaged by fire. It was installed atop the column in 1882.

The statue is on display for public viewing in the entrance hall of the Municipality of Lecce's headquarters, Palazzo Carafa, which is located nearby, while restoration work is being done. There is no guarantee that the repair work won't take another year. *Note: Restoration work is still ongoing.*

Amphitheatre in Rome

The Roman Amphitheatre is the Piazza Sant'Oronzoi's distinctive feature. It wasn't until the foundations of the modern Banca d'Italia building were being built almost a century ago that the remnants of this enormous structure were discovered.

 The site wasn't adequately excavated until after 1944, with just about half of it now visible and the remainder hidden beneath nearby structures. Everything is visible from the Piazza; in addition to the tiers of sitting, remnants of animal pens, etc., are also visible.

During its prime (1st and 2nd century AD), the amphitheatre could hold more than 24,000 spectators, which was comparatively tiny by historical standards. It held gladiator matches, savage animal battles, open executions, and other events. These days, it serves as the backdrop for Christmas nativity scenes and outdoor performances in the summer.

Roman Amphitheatre in Lecce

Not to be confused with the Amphitheatre, the Roman Theatre (Teatro Romano) is another important Roman structure located close to the Piazza Sant'Oronzo and the Piazza Duomo, but tucked away in side alleyways. This was unintentionally found in 1928 while doing some work in the gardens of some old palazzi nearby.

After that, it was excavated, and in 1989, a tiny museum was added.The public can visit the museum and theatre from Monday through Saturday from 9.00 am to 1 pm for 4 euros.

The theatre, which held many plays and other acts and could hold up to 6,000 people, was constructed in the first and second centuries and was a significant aspect of Roman Lecce. It is carved out of a stony valley. Prominent individuals were seated in a semicircular "orchestra" made of original stone slabs.

There are curtain channels and scenery recesses visible on the huge stage. There may be roughly 5,000 seats in the cavea (auditorium). It is constructed with limestone blocks that have been split into six sections by stairwells.

A few exhibits about Roman theatre in general as well as items like masks and costumes can be seen in the tiny museum. An intriguing model depicts what the entire theatre would have looked like.

Castello di Lecce

Near the Piazza Sant'Oronzo stands the Lecce Castle. This was constructed in the 1550s and was a part of the Puglian castle construction boom that Emperor Charles V ordered to protect the area from the Turks (Otranto and Copertino were also built during this period). Encircling a courtyard, it is a sizable and sturdy quadrilateral of bastions; the original moat and bridges were removed in 1873.

The castle, which was never required for defence, was used as a theatre, a barracks, and a residence. The local government took control of the castle in 1984 and made it the centre of Lecce's cultural services. These days,

Lecce is well-known for its papier-mache figure museum, festivals, and exhibitions.

There is a grand entrance gateway to the castle. The great, excavated central courtyard of the castle may be traversed on foot from the front to the back. You can also take a stroll around the outside to observe its dimensions and unique features. It costs 4 euros to enter, although the main reason is to view the exhibits, including the papier-mâché museum.

Three Gothic churches

This church might be the first significant baroque church a visitor encounters because it sits above a tiny piazza on Via Vittorio Emanuele, between Piazza Duomo and Piazza Sant'Oronzo. Built by Francesco Grimaldi of Turin between 1592 and 1638, it was devoted to Saint Irene of Lecce, the city's patron saint until Sant'Oronzo took over in 1657.

This was the church of the Theatines, a male monastic order that was disbanded in 1867 but whose edifice was preserved as a house of worship.

There are two portions to the façade. One of Lecce's most prominent baroque architects, Mauro Manieri, created a statue of Saint Irene in 1718, and vacant niches and sculpted scrolls divide the columns in the bottom half. The Lecce city seal is located above the longitudinal cornice that separates the two portions.

With a huge central window and a triangular uppermost unit (referred to as a "tympanum") topped with the emblems of the Theatine order and a Latin inscription honouring "Saint Irene - virgin and martyr," the upper section of the facade shares a pattern with the lower.

The church's interior is cross-shaped, with one nave and transept and around twelve chapels and altars. The entire thing is opulently embellished with sculptures, paintings, etc.

Santa Chiara's Church

The Roman Theatre is not far from this chapel. While work began in 1428. it wasn't completed until 1688-1692 when it was completely restored to its current state. The absence of the customary triangular top part gives the facade a rather shortened appearance. It is elaborately adorned with images of angels, vegetation, and religious symbols.

The coat of arms of the Santa Chiara order is displayed above the gateway, which is flanked by fluted columns. The bottom and top parts have a consistent pattern of vacant niches.

The church's seven huge windows let in a lot of natural light. The entire area is covered in sculptures, carved portraits, saint statues made of wood, and painted altars. Santa Chiara di Assisi is depicted in a statue on the majestic high altar.

Goddess of the Gods

This church served as the foundation for the Jesuits in Lecce after an ancient Greek Orthodox church on the property was destroyed in 1574. Over the course of the next 70 years or more, construction was done.

When compared to other churches in the area that were constructed a bit later, the facade's architecture is more understated. A straightforward design of pillars and vacant niches makes up the lowest portion. The Jesuit insignia is positioned above the doorway, with sculpted angels on either side.

Three windows and further decorative elements can be found in the upper half, which also has a little statue of the Child Jesus over the centre window. Religious imagery adorns the roof pediment, which is topped by a statue of a pelican—a common representation of a mother nursing her offspring.

There is a sizable nave inside, surrounded by a number of altars and chapels. All of these have important artworks and are deftly sculpted and designed. The Madonna del Buon Consiglio is the subject of a significant chapel (the church is sometimes referred to by this name).

But the big altar takes the stage. This was designed in the middle of the 17th century by Guiseppe Cino, who was a prominent Lecce architect at the period and was in charge of many of the structures that were constructed. Surrounded by sculpted twisted columns, it features a painting by Jacopo Robusti depicting the Circumcision.

Numerous statues, paintings, and sculpted figures combine to create a breathtaking whole impression.

The base's wooden (walnut) stalls, which date back to the 18th century, are tastefully adorned with flowers and other motifs.

Santa Croce Basilica

Many people believe that the Basilica di Santa Croce is the most significant baroque structure in all of Italy and represents the pinnacle of Puglian baroque architecture.

This dramatic spectacle is not to be missed by anyone visiting Lecce, especially its beautifully decorated facade, which is well worth examining in detail.

It is somewhat of a surprise as the street opens and the dramatic facade becomes visible because the church is situated on Via Umberto I, a narrow street that is only a short distance from Piazza Sant'Oronzo.

A protracted phase of renovation has been underway for the entire edifice. Before 2023, the facade was hidden behind sheeting and scaffolding during our visits, and there was occasionally restricted access within. But now that the construction is done, the church—including the facade—can be seen clearly.

The church was originally built in 1354, but the most of its building was done between 1549 and 1646 under the supervision of several prominent local architects, including Gabriele Riccardi, and Cesare Penna. The best masons, sculptors, and artists on the market at the period were involved. After the Jews were driven from the city in 1510, the buildings that had formed the centre of Lecce's Jewish district were demolished to construct the site.

The well-known facade merits close examination. It is helpful to have some background knowledge on it to aid in enjoyment, as it contains many historical allusions and important references.

Generally speaking, the facade of Santa Croce represents the victory of Christianity over paganism; this was particularly significant during the building period, when the Turks had only just been routed and driven out of this region of Europe. The lower portion symbolises the underworld, where mythological creatures like dragons, harpies, and sirens can be seen peeping out of the pediment and capitals.

The divine forces, depicted in the upper section of the facade with flowers, plants, animals, and angels, vanquish this profane earth.

The most ornate portion is the upper section, which was created by **Cesaro Penna** and features a balcony supported by gryphons, dragons, lions, and other animals. A rose window sits in the centre, surrounded by berries and bay leaves.

Two Corinthian columns, one on either side of the rose window, divide the central area from the flanks where niches holding statues of Pope Celestine V and St. Benedict are located. However, two sizable statues of women—Faith and Fortitude—stand on either side of the façade.

Some analysts view the facade as a particular commemoration of the 16th century Battle of Lepanto victory. After the Ottoman Empire was vanquished by the Western forces in this conflict, Salento, then known as Terra d'Otranto, which had previously been under continual Saracen siege, benefited greatly economically and commercially.

The male faces, known as telamons, disguised as Turks serve as a reminder of the captives taken during the conflict by the formidable Venetian fleet. The creatures shown in the balustrade are symbolic of the allied Christian powers: the gryphon represents Genoa; the dragon represents the Boncompagni dynasty, of whom

Pope Gregory XIII was a member; and the Hercules represents the Grand Duke of Tuscany.

Evenings and mornings are available to the public at the Basilica. A lofty nave is surrounded by aisles that house sixteen chapels, each of which is recognised as a masterpiece of baroque sculpture and painting.

The chapel dedicated to San Francesco di Paulo, located on the left aisle, is the most significant artistically. This was created in 1615–16 by Francesco Antonio Zimbalo and features an altar in the centre surrounded by ornate columns. Twelve carved panels that depict the saint's life are positioned between the columns, and sculptures of angels and other symbols crown the entire structure.

The Palazzo Celestini, a crucial component of the complex planned by Gabriele Riccardi, is located next to the Basilica Santa Croce. Specifically for the Celestine monastic order, this was created. Commencing in 1548, the construction of the Basilica took more than a century to complete.
The lengthy stretch on Via Umberto I was constructed between 1658 and 1694, following the ideas of renowned Lecce architect Guiseppe Cino and Giuiseppe Zimbalo.

The Palazzo, also known as the Palazzo della Provincia, was commandeered as a public structure following the suppression of the monastic order in 1807 and today serves as the home of the provincial offices of Lecce.

The facade is a magnificent exhibition of windows, ornamental elements, and columns. In addition, there is a charming patio within.

Public Parks

The Public Gardens, which have trees and fountains, are accessible by strolling via the Palazzo dei Celestini courtyard. These can provide much-needed reprieve from the summertime heat of Lecce's streets.

The Jewish museum of Lecce is located in Palazzo Taurino.

If you're not a die-hard baroque fan, Lecce is a good area to meander around and visit on a more relaxed basis. Of course, there are numerous galleries and museums. A recent and somewhat out of the ordinary addition to these is a museum housed in the Palazzo Taurino, close to Santa Croce, that depicts the Jewish contribution to mediaeval Lecce.

It offers an insight into life in the city before the baroque era, when Jews played a significant role in its trade and economic prosperity. Remains of baths supplied by the watercourse beneath the city can be found at the location, which is in the basement of an old synagogue.

There are multilingual tours available. A short film tells the story of the camps established in this region of Italy in 1945 to house Jews who had survived the Holocaust before they relocated, primarily to Israel and America.

My Trip

Lecce is frequently referred to as South Italy's Florence. I ended up spending a full month there in Puglia.

Italy's next travel destination is Puglia. Puglia was previously a well-liked holiday destination for Italians, but now it's gaining attention from other countries as well. It is a must-visit location on my itinerary for my road trip through Italy.

This is a result of the fact that too many people have already been to Tuscany, the Amalfi Coast, or the canal cities, and they are looking for something fresh.

You would therefore adore Lecce if, like me, you prefer simpler travel places free of throngs of people yet are nevertheless hopelessly romantic at heart and adore old streets.

Does Lecce merit a visit, then? Indeed, this baroque treasure located on the southeast heel of Italy is a fantastic travel location, and I'll explain why.

Lecce is the ideal city for aimless strolling and getting lost. There are many fascinating stores and homes along the beautiful streets.

The best thing about strolling about Lecce's streets was that, because of the architecture of the homes lining the streets, the majority of the area was shaded even during the hottest part of the summer. Thus, the shade was really helpful even though it was about 36–39 degrees in Salento in August when I visited.

After exploring the old streets for a while, unwind at one of the cafes with outside seating that opens into the charming cobblestone pathways.

Unlike the inner streets that I fell in love with and took pictures of, Lecce's Old Town main street was packed. Vendors selling unique handcrafted goods that are found in many European tourist destinations line both sides of the main thoroughfare. Even though I didn't particularly enjoy this street, I still wanted to let you know.

There are numerous historic structures in Lecce.

Lecce boasts a stunning old town filled with historically significant Baroque buildings. The "Lecce Stone"—have you heard of it? Lecce is well-known for its well-known limestone, which is exported for sculpting all over the world. This Lecce Stone is used in the construction of Lecce's buildings.

Barocco leccese, or Lecce baroque, is the name given to the architectural style of this city. Anticipate to see an abundance of finely detailed carvings on every element of the historic buildings, including arches, columns, and gargoyles.

The Roman amphitheatre at Lecce is from the second century, just like the one in Rome.
The Italian city of Lecce's Roman Amphitheatre Ruins
I don't expect you to see every ancient structure and landmark in Lecce, but you may observe many of them from the outside as you stroll around the city's historical centre.

I've highlighted a few things in Lecce that you should keep an eye out for when exploring the old town.
In the centre of Lecce's historical district sits a mediaeval amphitheatre. It is as old as the second century, as I have already indicated, but here's the insane part.

Anfiteatro Romano was always concealed but was only uncovered in the early 20th century. Only half of the structure was dug up because the other half was occupied by a building.

Explore it and take in this superbly conserved historical artefact. You will like taking pictures of this sunken amphitheatre from unique perspectives.

Sant'Oronzo Square

Within the historic baroque town is the city square known as Piazza Sant'Oronzo. Among the many intriguing landmarks in this plaza is a statue of Sant'Oronzo. It includes the Roman Amphitheatre. You'll come across numerous fascinating engravings made from Lecce stone, a white limestone.

Practically every street in Lecce's ancient district leads to Piazza S. Oronzo if you stroll around it.

Santa Croce Basilica

Lecce's most well-known historical church, the Basilica di Santa Croce, was built in the 1620s. Not only does it have remarkable exterior architecture, but it also showcases superb interior Baroque design. In Florence, there's also a renowned church with the same name!

The elaborate figurines and circular window on the exterior are only a few of the many details. Marchese Grimaldi claimed that the Basilica di Santa Croce's exterior resembled a madman dreaming. I'm not sure about you, but remarks like these pique my interest much!

The Basilica di Santa Croce took 150 years to finish, thanks to three rival artists. The price of entry is 7 EUR, however it's well worth it for the beautiful interior design and paintings within. Inside, the basilica is incredibly serene.

Lecce Cathedral + Bell Tower

The Lecce Cathedral, or Duomo di Lecce in English, was constructed in 1143 and reconstructed in 1658. The structure is devoted to the Virgin Mary, as shown by its full name, Cattedrale Maria Santissima Assunta e S.Oronzo.
The Piazza leads to the centre, where you can find the Duomo di Lecce. You can see the bell tower of this cathedral from a distance.

The Duomo di Lecce, like many other churches in the area, has an ornate exterior. Numerous columns are embellished with figures of ascending angels.

The stained glass image of the Virgin Mary and the triangle with an eye within will appeal to Dan Brown fans.

Porta Napoli

The historic arch known as Porta Napoli formerly served as Lecce's walled city gate. Stroll around it and take in your surroundings.

Instead of attempting to catch the entire arch with your click, utilise it as a frame and click through it to create an amazing photo.

In addition to the locations listed above, the historical centre of Lecce is home to numerous churches and historical sites, including the **Paisiello Theatre**, Santa Chiara (the Church of Saint Clare), and the Obelisk (Obelisco).

Select a few landmarks to visit during your vacation, as you cannot see them all, like in Rome or Florence.

Enjoy a Rest in Parco Giochi & Giardini Pubblici Giuseppe Garibaldi

Why would I put a public park on such a list? That's because I'm giving you reasons to go to Lecce, and since the city is extravagant in every way, even the city park is extravagant.

Make sure to take a stop in the beautiful municipal park in Lecce. The kids will appreciate it if you are taking them on a trip. You won't miss it because it is directly adjacent to the Basilica of Santa Croce.

Giardini Pubblici Giuseppe Garibaldi, a public park in Lecce, has a fountain, lots of trees, plants, and benches. Bring some light fare, such as calzones and arancini, and have a picnic here.

Children will appreciate you taking them here if you are travelling with them because this park, Parco Giochi, includes an indoor playground.

You could easily spend an hour or so with small children in this park because there are plenty of benches and activities for them to do.

What makes visiting a new place the finest aspect of travel? For me, it involves sampling local cuisine that is exclusive to that location. Lecce did not let me down in this regard.

Cozze Gratin, or Parmesan-baked mussels, is a dish from Puglia, Italy.

I've had mussels in a lot of different places throughout the world, but the ones in Italy taste the finest. I recently tasted a different version of this that was really delicious and included prawns and squid.

Naturally, Puglia's extensive coastline on three sides contributes to the region's abundance of fresh fish.

Pasta with Frutti di Mare - Seafood Italian Puglia pasta
The Italian term for seafood is "Frutti di Mare," which means "fruits of the sea." Expect the tastiest pizzas, pastas, and Frutti di Mare risottos when visiting Puglia. My usual dinner in Salento was frutta di mare linguine.

Gelato breaks are required in Lecce, Italy.
Gelato is always a good choice, and Lecce Old Town has some fantastic gelato businesses. I used to get coffee gelato a lot since I enjoyed the cool taste. My daughter and hubby chose the delicious flavours. I enjoyed the delicious flavours so much that I returned for more.

Enjoy Wine and Typical Italian Summer Nights
How can one maximise their time in a lovely location such as Lecce? Have a romantic dinner and a glass of wine at one of the eateries with outside seating.

If you want to enjoy antipasti and wine the Italian way, you will sit for as long as possible. You might ask your server for suggestions on the fresh catch of the day for supper as the evening wears on.

Although the summer is not the ideal season for red wine, I heartily suggest Puglia's Primitivo reds; they are a great choice. Prosecco is a great option, of course, if you're searching for something sparkling.

Those who enjoy white wine ought to try Moscatello Selvatico. I've had the Rosè Salento wine a few times; it's simply named Rosè Salento and it was incredibly refreshing.

Visit Torre Sant'Andrea as a Side Trip
One of my favourite beaches in Salento is only 20–35 kilometres from Lecce. We refer to it as Torre Sant'Andrea. In my opinion, this is Puglia's most gorgeous beach, and I'm glad I was able to visit it.

If you want to see any of Puglia while road touring across Italy, you absolutely must stop at Torre Sant'Andrea.
The tiny, sandy section of Torre Sant'Andrea beach resembles a paradise. This place has very clear, turquoise-blue, and refreshing water. The sand is flawless and velvety.

The archways and rock formations, known as I Faraglioni di Sant'Andrea, is where the beach really shines, however you have to cross the rocks and take a little stroll to get there. (Much like the Portuguese Algarve beaches.)

The rock formations and arches of Sant'Andrea, Puglia's I Faraglioni di Sant'Andrea

The views are wonderful on the trek over the rocks to get to the arches from the sandy beach. As you trek towards the arches, there's also a food truck perched atop the rocks selling reasonably priced munchies.

Without hiking shoes, we tried this with our 3-year-old daughter, and it worked. You must exercise extreme caution while doing this with young children as they could get hurt if they fall.

The Numerous Locations for Swimming and Cliff Jumping at Torre Sant'Andrea Puglia
This place has a lot of folks who leap off cliffs. We decided not to cliff jump because we were here with our kid, even though the water was incredibly clear.

It only took us thirty minutes to drive from Lecce to Torre Sant'Andrea, but parking here was a problem. When we finally did, it was unshadowed.

Grotta della Poesia, or the Cave of Poetry, is another breathtaking spot along the coast close to Lecce. Not too far away is Torre Sant'Andrea. The outing was already too long for my toddler, so I was unable to go, but I hope you were able to.

How do I get to Lecce from Bari?

Bari is not as near to Brindisi as Lecce is. If you wish to visit Salento (the heel of the boot of Italy), you can fly directly to Brindisi rather than Bari because it also has an airport.

Local transit can take you from Lecce to Bari. Proceed to the Bari Centrale station, from where buses to Lecce Stazione depart several times daily.
These buses depart Bari and arrive in Lecce around two hours later. En route, they make a stop in Brindisi. You'll get to see beautiful scenery on the bus route along the coast of Salento.

If you're driving in Italy, you can use the beautiful SS16 highway that hugs the shore to get from Bari to Lecce.

There are many old olive trees, numerous vine farms, and prickly pear cactuses that have grown into enormous trees if you choose to escape the highway by using the smaller interior paths.

Lecce Travel

The train station in Lecce is located south of the city centre, one kilometre (1 hour's walk) from Piazza del Duomo. Trains travel an hour and fifty-three minutes from Lecce to Bari (Bari Centrale), making stops at Brindisi (27 minutes), Ostuni (52 minutes), Cisternino (58 minutes), Monopoli (1 hour 15 minutes), and Polignano a Mare (1 hour 2w minutes).

It's better to take a bus to the well-known coastal village of Gallipoli on the Ionian shore; a number 108 will take you there in 48 minutes.

The closest airport to Lecce is Brindisi Salento Airport, which is 48 km away and 33 minutes by vehicle. Bari Karol Wojtyla Airport is the next best choice, taking an hour and forty-five minutes to get there (168 km).

Public transport: local buses and the central train station
  - By car: 1 hour 17 minutes (108 km), 31 minutes (39 km) to Brindisi
Travel time to get to Brindisi Salento Airport: 34 minutes (47 km) by vehicle

  - By rail: Cisternino - 59 minutes, Ostuni - 51 minutes, Brindisi - 28 minutes

Tourist Office in Lecce Italy

Infotab - Lecce Walking Tours
Tourist information centre in Lecce, Italy
Address: Via Umberto I, 18, 73100 Lecce LE, Italy
Phone: +39 328 948 2091

Tourist Information Centre, Piazza Del Duomo
Address: Servizio OnLine, 73100 Lecce LE, Italy
Phone: +39 0832 179 2778

Info Lecce
Tourist information centre in Lecce, Italy
Address: P.za del Duomo, 2, 73100 Lecce LE, Italy
Phone: +39 0832 521877

Attractions

Below are more Attractions in the city, both popular and lesser-known ones. Visit any of them, depending on your preference.

- - Castello Carlo V
  - Location: Via XXV Luglio
  Medieval castle hosting events, a historical landmark that captivates visitors with its medieval charm.

- - Museo Faggiano
  - Location: Via Ascanio Grandi, 56/58
  Archaeological site beneath a contemporary home, offering a unique glimpse into history hidden beneath modern architecture.

- - Railway Museum of Puglia
  - Location: Via G. Codacci Pisanelli, 3
  Fascinating museum showcasing the history of railways in Puglia, a must-visit for enthusiasts and history buffs.

- - Basilica di Santa Croce
  - Location: Via Umberto I, 1
  1600s church with an intricate facade, a testament to historical architecture and religious significance.

- - Torre di Belloluogo
  - Location: Via Vecchia Surbo, 48

Historical site offering a rich exploration, a place resonating with the echoes of its storied past.

- • - MUST (Museo Storico Città di Lecce)
- Location: Via Degli Ammirati, 11
Engaging museum with captivating exhibits, providing a journey through the storied history of Lecce.

- • - Mura urbiche
- Location: Viale Michele de Pietro, 10
Historical monuments and memorials, reflecting the rich cultural and historical tapestry of the city.

- • - Ex Convento degli Agostiniani
- Location: Viale Michele de Pietro, 10
Former Augustinian convent with historical significance, an architectural gem contributing to the city's cultural heritage.

- • - Palazzo Turrisi-Palumbo
- Location: Via Marco Basseo, 16
Historical palace showcasing architectural grandeur, a testament to the opulence of the past.

- • - Museo Diocesano di Arte Sacra
- Location: P.za del Duomo, 5
Intriguing museum with a rich history of sacred art, providing insight into the city's religious and artistic heritage.

- • - Fontana Dell'Armonia

- Location: Via G. Marconi, 45
Harmonious fountain blending art and architecture, a serene spot contributing to the city's aesthetic appeal.

- • - Palazzo Guarini
- Location: Via Giuseppe Palmieri, 4
Historic palace with architectural significance, adding to the charm of Lecce's cultural landscape.

- • - Teatro Romano
- Location: Via Del Teatro Romano
Roman theater with an adjoining museum, a historical site that brings ancient entertainment to life.

- • - Jewish Museum Lecce
- Location: Via Umberto I, 9
Museum chronicling the city's Jewish history, a valuable exploration of cultural diversity and historical narratives.

- • - Ex Chiesa di San Marco
- Location: Piazza Sant'Oronzo, 41
Former church with historical significance, a site resonating with the city's religious and cultural past.

- • - Parco di Belloluogo
- Location: Via Vecchia Surbo, 1d
Playful park offering a space for kids to explore and enjoy, blending recreational activities with natural surroundings.

- • - Porta Rudiae
- Location: Via Gorizia, 18

  Ornamental gate leading to the old city, a historical entry point showcasing intricate craftsmanship.

- • - Palazzo Marrese
- Location: Piazzeta Ignazio Falconieri, 2-6

  Historical palace contributing to the city's architectural legacy, an elegant structure with cultural significance.

- • - Campanile del Duomo
- Location: P.za del Duomo

  Cathedral bell tower with historical importance, a prominent feature in the city's skyline.

- • - Arco di Prato
- Location: Piazzetta Arco di Prato, 18

  Arch with historical significance, a notable landmark embodying the city's architectural heritage.

Leisure Activities

Below are activities to get involved in, suggestions on day trips and excursions, Embark on any of these activities to enhance your travel experience.

- - Orecchiette Cooking Class and Wine Tasting: Immerse yourself in the culinary delights of Lecce with a hands-on orecchiette pasta cooking class paired with a delightful wine tasting experience.

- - Tour to 4 Towns of Salento (Otranto, Leuca, Gallipoli, Galatina): Embark on a 4WD adventure exploring the charm and history of Salento, visiting picturesque towns like Otranto, Leuca, Gallipoli, and Galatina.

- - Lecce History and Street Food Tasting Tour: Discover the rich history of Lecce while indulging in its delectable street food. A guided tour that combines cultural insights with tasty local treats.

- - Otranto and Castro Full-Day Tour: Join a bus tour to explore the scenic beauty of Otranto and Castro, discovering historical landmarks and enjoying the coastal charm of these enchanting towns.

- - Valley D'itria Full Day Tour (Cisternino, Alberobello, Polignano a Mare): Traverse the beautiful Valley D'itria on a bus tour, exploring the charming villages of Cisternino and Alberobello, and ending the day in the coastal gem, Polignano a Mare.

- - Visit to ALBEROBELLO & MATERA from Lecce or province: Embark on a full-day tour from Lecce to the unique towns of Alberobello and Matera, discovering the fascinating history and architecture of these UNESCO World Heritage Sites.

- - 1 Hour Private Lesson of Pizzica, Traditional Dance of Salento: Dive into the cultural heritage of Salento with a private lesson in Pizzica, a traditional dance, offering a glimpse into the region's vibrant folklore.

41

- - Jewish Museum Lecce - 45 minutes Private Guided Tour: Explore the rich history of Lecce's Jewish community with a private guided tour of the Jewish Museum, delving into centuries of cultural heritage.

- - Lecce: Baroque and Underground Tour - Private Tour: Uncover the architectural wonders of Lecce with a private tour, exploring its Baroque gems above ground and delving into fascinating underground sites.

- - Full Day Tour of Otranto City and its Amazing Seacoast from Lecce: Experience the allure of Otranto and its stunning seacoast on a full-day tour from Lecce, immersing yourself in the history and beauty of this coastal gem.

When travelling, it's advisable to book your tours in advance if interested. Consider using Viator (https://www.viator.com/) for great deals. Scan the QR code to book online.

General information

Emergency Numbers: Dial 112 for all-hazards help.
- 113 (accidents, thefts, and police problems).
- Fire Department: 115 (for fire emergencies and weather-related difficulties).
- Urgent Medical Attention: 118 (for medical crises or mountain or cave rescue).
- Roadside Assistance (ACI): 803.116.

To call Italy, dial the international code +39 followed by the number.
- To make an international call from Italy, dial 00 followed by the international code and number.

Purchasing an Italian SIM card for cost-effective communication is recommended.

Tips
- Exercise care at night, at train stations, airports, and in congested places.
- Be on the lookout for pickpockets, especially if they seem to be well-dressed.
- Be cautious while drinking extensively to prevent being a victim of crime.

Packing Suggestions
Best Luggage & Bags: - A hard-sided suitcase for long-term use.
   - For carry-on, a sturdy backpack or a lightweight shoulder bag.
   - A fashionable crossbody bag for tiny necessities.
   - A tote bag made of canvas or mesh for adaptability.

What to Bring in Your Carry-On Bag
  - A valid passport and, if necessary, a visa.
  - Cash and credit cards are accepted.
  - An extra pair of pants for unexpected layovers.

Headphones or noise-cancelling earphones are recommended for in-flight use.
  - A sleep mask to help you sleep throughout the journey.
  - A shawl, pashmina, or travel blanket to keep you warm.
  - For amusement, use an iPad or a lightweight laptop.

Basic One-Week Packing List
  - A variety of tank tops, tees, blouses, and long-sleeve tops.
  - Jeans, black or neutral trousers and a lightweight jacket are all appropriate.
  - Pants, yoga pants and sweatshirts.
  - Sneakers and more formal shoes, sunglasses and a water bottle.

Seasonal Additions
-**Spring**: raincoat, scarves and a travel umbrella.
  Summer attire includes sundresses, shorts, swimsuits, flip-flops and sunscreen.
  - In the **autumn**, bring a warm hat, scarf, additional layers, a travel umbrella and boots.
  - In the **winter**, bring a winter coat, additional layers, gloves, and toiletries.

Packing toiletries for pain alleviation, constipation, diarrhoea, and motion sickness.

What NOT to Bring
Valuables and expensive jewellery to prevent pickpocketing.
   - Full-sized toiletries; choose travel-sized or half-used goods instead.
   - Hairdryer and heat styling gadgets; most hotels provide them.

Last but not least, pack smartly with appropriate footwear and gear for the season.
- Have a wonderful time in Italy.

Planning
Best Time to Visit: From April to June, the weather is great, avoiding the sweltering heat of summer. Late spring has a bright sky and less people.

Considerations for Summer: July and August are peak months, with crowded beaches and increased pricing. Prepare for hot weather by planning and booking ahead of time.

Autumn Delights: From September to November, the weather is mild and the landscape is beautiful. Take advantage of cuisine festivals, wine harvests, and cultural activities.

Winter Attractions: Snow activities are popular in the Alps from December to March. Winter also offers Christmas markets, New Year's Eve events, and reduced off-season travel expenses.

Practical Information

Holiday Season: Italians often travel on vacation in August, resulting in crowded beaches, business closures, and increased pricing. Plan ahead of time, particularly near Ferragosto on August 15.

While Italy is a car-centric country, public transit is both economical and dependable. Renting a vehicle allows independence, yet trains and buses successfully link major centres.

Car Rental scarcity: Due to the pandemic, there is a rental car scarcity. Book early, particularly during high holiday seasons.

Card payments are typically accepted, however bringing cash is recommended for occasional outliers. The majority of major credit card networks are accepted.

Regional Pride: Celebrate regional pride (campanilismo) by learning about how inhabitants take pride in their own locations, which provide unique experiences and flavours.

Sarcasm in Humour: Sarcasm and self-deprecation are often used in Italian humour. Expect clever conversation, particularly in locations such as Veneto or Tuscany.

Hand Gestures: Italians use expressive hand gestures to communicate. Learn the meanings of the gestures to prevent misunderstandings, since each gesture carries different information.

Restaurant Etiquette: Don't be intimidated by lengthy

menus. You are not required to order from each area. You may mix and combine dishes as you want.

Tipping Culture: Tipping is not required, although it is appreciated for outstanding service. Some restaurants may levy "coperto" fees.

Timing of Eating and Drinking: Stick to local conventions such as drinking a coffee in the morning, an Aperol Spritz before dinner, and limoncello after meals. Lunch is served at 1pm, while supper is served around 8pm.

Drinking in Public: Drinking alcohol in public is legal and widespread in many places. Outdoor drinking, particularly in public squares, is an important aspect of local social life.

Cheek Kissing Etiquette: In casual contexts, Italians often greet with cheek kisses. Pay attention to social clues, and if you're uneasy, a simple handshake will be enough.

Political Awareness: Political polarisation is increasing in Italy. Be cognizant of opposing viewpoints, particularly in conversations like migration, energy, housing, and workers' rights. Political debates may be heated, so read the room appropriately.

Budget Travel in Italy
Fly into minor airports provided by low-cost airlines; consider alternate transit choices, such as high-speed trains linking big cities.

Travel during the shoulder seasons (May, June,

September, and October) to balance weather, prices, and avoid peak crowds.

Taking Public transit vs Renting a Car: Taking public transit is a more cost-effective option to explore cities.
  - Save money by purchasing high-speed rail tickets in advance, and think about multi-day travel passes.

Affordable Dining: For low-cost lunches, look for fixed-price lunch menus at trattorias.
  - To avoid extra service costs, order your espresso at the bar.

Water and Beverages: Drink tap water to save money and limit your use of plastic.
  - When sitting at cafés, be in mind that service costs may apply.

Art & Cultural Exploration: Schedule art excursions during off-seasons to save money on museum admission.
  - Visit churches to see free exhibits of famous artworks.

- Look for "free" beaches (spiaggia libera) to avoid paying rental fees at private beaches.
  - Ask around for information on free beach places that are accessible.

Pilgrimages on a Budget: Consider hiking or bicycling along traditional pilgrimage routes such as the Via Francigena.
  - For less expensive lodging, stay in monasteries or pilgrim hostels.

Average Daily Costs: - Budget at least €130 a day to cover key attractions, lunches, and transportation.

Alternative Lodging Options: - Look into low-cost options such as hostels or agriturismi (farm stays). - For multi-day rail travel, use the **Trenitalia Pass**.

Off-Peak Art Exploration: During the off-season, prominent art institutions offer cheap admission.

Transportation Savings Tip
Fly with low-cost carriers such as **Ryanair, WizzAir, EasyJet, or Vueling**. - Consider overland entrance or intercity travel via high-speed trains.

Environmental and financial savings may be obtained by drinking tap water and avoiding the use of single-use plastics.

Exploring Italy on a budget entails making smart decisions about travel seasons, means of transportation, food alternatives, and cultural discovery to ensure a cheap but meaningful trip.

Transportation and Visa

Visas are not required for citizens of Schengen nations, the EU, or the EAA.

- Around 60 non-EU countries, including the United Kingdom, the United States, Canada, Japan, Australia, and others, have visa-free travel for up to 90 days during any 180-day period.

- Other countries need a Schengen visa; application procedures differ.

Working Holiday Visa: Italy grants working holiday visas to young people aged 18 to 30 from Australia, Japan, New Zealand, South Korea, and Canada.

Local Transportation: - Trenitalia and Italo maintain an extensive rail network linking key cities in Italy.
   - Buses serve regions that are not served by trains, while long-distance coaches are controlled by commercial firms such as **Flixbus**.
   - Ferries are used to link islands and coastal regions.

Driving in Italy: - Renting a car, motorbike or Vespa provides freedom, particularly in rural regions.
   - Roads are divided into several groups with varied speed restrictions.
   - Potholes, traffic, and parking issues are all possible driving circumstances.

Domestic flights are possible, however they are often less convenient than trains or buses.
   - Airlines such as ITA Airways, easyJet, and Ryanair fly into major cities.

Cycling: Cycling pathways, including electric bike alternatives, are available throughout Italy.
   - Road cycling is popular in Northern Italy, particularly in the Alps and Dolomites.

Accessibility: While Italy is developing accessibility, there are still obstacles for impaired travellers.
   - Some trains and buses provide help to disabled passengers.

> **- Village for All and Fondazione Cesare Serono** are two online organisations that give information about accessible amenities and beaches.

Do you know?

The top Two Restaurants in Italy are Chefs Massimo Bottura (Osteria Francescana) and Niko Romito (Reale)

Tourists throws more than €1,000,000 into the Trevi Fountain each year

Pizza was invented in Naples

Italy is the world's largest wine producer

It's bad Omen to place bread upside down on the table.

Common hand gestures in Italy

- Raised Index Finger: Used to get someone's attention or emphasize a point.

- Chin Flick: A quick flick of the chin with the fingers, often used to express indifference or dismissal.

- Hand Purse (Fingers Kissing): Fingers brought together in a kissing motion, indicating perfection, excellence, or approval.

- Thumb and Fingers Pinched Together: Signifying that something is expensive or costly.

- Clenched Fist with Raised Arm: A gesture of victory or success.

- Cheek Pinch: Gently pinching the cheek of a child or someone close as a sign of affection.

- Shrugging Shoulders: A universal gesture of expressing uncertainty or not knowing.

- Italian Hand Gesture (Fingers Together, Shaking Side to Side): Expressing uncertainty, disbelief, or disagreement.

- Hand on Heart: Placing the hand on the chest to emphasize sincerity or truthfulness.

Scan the QR code below and search for the Location you are going to in Italy and have a better view. Safe travels.

The map is the same on your phone. Consider taking screenshots as you walk around with no connection needed. Alternatively, you can contact the tourist office using the addresses and numbers provided in this guide.

Write down your activities in the box below

Day 1	Day 2	Day 3
Arrival (hotel) and Acquaintance	Adventure (leisure) and relaxation	Explore and Farewell

Write down your activities in the box below

Day 4	Day 5	Day 6
Arrival (hotel) and Acquaintance	Adventure (leisure) and relaxation	Explore and Farewell

In most cases, I use the Wanderlog website or app to plan my trip itinerary and expenses. You can try it if you're interested. Click the link below or scan the QR code to create a new account.

https://wanderlog.com

Transportation
Below are recommended Transportation related services in the city. It is advisable to make reservations online at **omio.com** or by scanning the QR code.

Transport Services

Below are recommended transportation-related services in the city. Contact them if necessary upon landing at the nearby airport. It is advisable to make reservations online at omio.com or by scanning the QR code above.

- - AnTour Shuttle
- Type: Minibus taxi service
- Address: Piazza Sant'Oronzo, 1
- Phone: +39 389 569 5280

- - Fast Shuttle NCC - Taxi Transfer e Noleggio con Conducente
- Type: Taxi service
- Address: Via de Nicola Enrico, 14
- Phone: +39 338 830 8132

- - Servizio Navetta aeroporto Lecceauto.It Srl
- Type: Airport shuttle service
- Address: Cavallino, Province of Lecce, Italy
- Phone: +39 329 905 9433

- - GRtransfer
- Type: Transportation service
- Phone: +39 388 752 5121

- - NCC LECCE - Taurino Shuttle
- Type: Transportation escort service
- Phone: +39 328 733 4495

- - Taxi 12 Lecce
- Type: Taxi service
- Address: Viale G. Leopardi, 52
- Phone: +39 349 358 6599

- - Servizio Taxi 10 Lecce
- Type: Taxi service
- Address: Via Don Bosco, 26
- Phone: +39 329 385 9770

- - RADIO TAXI del Comune di Lecce
- Type: Taxi service
- Address: Via Garigliano, 5
- Phone: +39 0832 1779

- - Navetta Brindisi Lecce, Prezzi - Transfer - NCC
- Type: Minibus taxi service
- Phone: +39 329 376 7714

- - Transfer stazione Lecce simil Taxi
- Type: Taxi service
- Address: Via Enrico Bozzi, 15
- Phone: +39 320 863 0095

- - Cooperativa TAXI LECCE
- Type: Taxis
- Address: Via Paolo Colaci, 55
- Phone: +39 328 671 4428

- - TAXI & NCC LECCE

- Type: Taxi service
- Address: Via Reno, 2
- Phone: +39 393 030 6000

- • - Air Shuttle
- Type: Transportation service
- Address: Via Antonio Gramsci, 2
- Phone: +39 0832 305522

- • - Andrea Martina NCC Noleggio con conducente
  Transfer Service Brindisi, Lecce, Taranto
- Type: Transportation escort service
- Address: Via dei Palumbo, 49
- Phone: +39 331 222 1562

- • - Zemove
- Type: Transportation service
- Address: Via Corte dei Mesagnesi, 30 c
- Phone: +39 320 302 0113

- • - Salento in bus
- Type: Transportation service
- Address: Viale Gallipoli, 26 A

- • - Lecce - City Terminal Piazza carmelo bene
- Type: Bus stop
- Address: Piazza carmelo bene

Hotels

When traveling, it's advisable to book your hotel in advance.

Consider using Booking.com for great deals, available for select hotels worldwide. Scan the QR code to book online. Here are some recommended hotels to consider:

- • - Grand Hotel Di Lecce
- Location: Viale Oronzo Quarta, 28
- Phone: +39 0832 309405

Refined hotel with intricate decor, a bar, and a seasonal outdoor pool, offering a luxurious stay.

- • - Grand Hotel Tiziano e dei Congressi
- Location: Via Porta d'Europa
- Phone: +39 0832 272111

Relaxed hotel with unassuming rooms, free breakfast, a restaurant, and 2 bars, providing a comfortable retreat.

- **- Hotel delle Palme**
  - Location: Via di Leuca, 90
  - Phone: +39 0832 347171

  Relaxed hotel with straightforward rooms, a bar, a restaurant, and breakfast, ensuring a pleasant and easygoing stay.

- **- Risorgimento Resort**
  - Location: Via Augusto Imperatore, 19
  - Phone: +39 0832 246311

  Elegant hotel with plush quarters, a posh spa, an upscale restaurant, and a gym, promising a luxurious experience.

- **- Eos Hotel - VESTAS Hotels & Resorts**
  - Location: Viale Vittorio Alfieri, 11
  - Phone: +39 0832 230030

  Understated hotel with complimentary Wi-Fi and breakfast, featuring a coffee and wine bar for a relaxed stay.

- **- La Fiermontina**
  - Location: Piazzetta De Summa Scipione, 4
  - Phone: +39 0832 179 5982

  Refined hotel in a 17th-century home, offering an upscale restaurant and an outdoor pool for a sophisticated retreat.

- **- 8piuhotel**
  - Location: Viale del Risorgimento
  - Phone: +39 0832 306686

Chic, retro-inspired quarters in a hip hotel with free breakfast, a bar, and a modern restaurant, ensuring a stylish stay.

- • - Hilton Garden Inn Lecce
- Location: Via Cosimo de Giorgi, 62
- Phone: +39 0832 5252

Polished quarters with city views, in a contemporary hotel featuring a rooftop pool and a spa for a luxurious experience.

- • - Masseria & SPA Luciagiovanni
- Location: Via Antonio Fogazzaro
- Phone: +39 0832 179 1831

Upmarket Moorish-style pick with a restaurant, 2 pools, and a high-tech medical spa, offering a rejuvenating retreat.

- • - Torre del Parco
- Location: 1419, Viale Torre del Parco, 1
- Phone: +39 0832 347694

Restored medieval tower featuring original frescoes, a garden terrace, and a spa, offering a unique historical experience.

Restaurants

Try any of the top recommended restaurants known for their pleasant services, mouthwatering menus, and reasonable prices. You can reach them through the provided contact details.

- - 63 Osteria Contemporanea
- Location: Viale dell' Università, 63
- Phone: +39 393 133 3030
    Contemporary osteria crafting local delicacies like Orecchiette with rich tomato sauce and Taralli as crunchy appetizers.

- - 00 Doppiozero
- Location: Via Guglielmo Paladini, 2
- Phone: +39 0832 521052

Rustic-chic hub featuring Ciceri e Tria, a traditional Puglian dish blending chickpeas, pasta, and savory flavors.

- • - Mad
  - Location: Via Ludovico Maremonti
  - Phone: +39 329 963 4489

A unique blend of avant-garde cuisine at Mad, presenting Gnummareddi, fried dough fritters with anise flavor.

- • - Messapia Wine Bar
  - Location: Via Giacomo Matteotti, 6
  - Phone: +39 328 656 2966

Italian classics like Puccia, round bread stuffed with cured meats and cheese, offered in a cozy atmosphere.

- • - Alex
  - Location: Via Vito Fazzi, 15/23
  - Phone: +39 320 803 4258

Elegant seafood at Alex, featuring Octopus Salad, a cold salad with tender octopus and fresh ingredients.

- • - Osteria di Lecce
  - Location: Via Liborio Romano, 37
  - Phone: +39 327 539 2935

Homestyle dishes like Frise, twice-baked bread served with fresh tomatoes and olive oil.

- • - I Latini
  - Location: Via Giuseppe Palmieri, 46

- Phone: +39 0832 524578
Cozy stop for regional cuisine, offering Panzerotti, turnovers filled with tomato and mozzarella, fried to perfection.

- • - OSTERIA 203
- Location: Viale Francesco Lo Re, 39
- Phone: +39 339 870 1468
Homey venue serving signature Puglian dishes like Tiella, a flavorful casserole with layers of rice, potatoes, and mussels.

- • - Il Vico Del Gusto • Ristorante
- Location: Vico dei Fieschi, 14
- Phone: +39 0832 246931
Refined seafood in upscale surroundings, featuring Burrata, a creamy cheese delicacy with a soft centre.

- • - La Dogana Bistrot Lecce - Ristorante di pesce
- Location: Viale della libertà, 93
- Phone: +39 0832 401054
Fish restaurant offering Orecchiette, a signature pasta served with broccoli rabe and local ingredients.

- • - Pietrabianca Vino e Cucina
- Location: Via Benedetto Cairoli, 25
- Phone: +39 0832 300456
Dine-in spot featuring classics like Taralli, ring-shaped snacks flavored with fennel, black pepper, or chili.

- • - Bacaro & Zio Pesce Osteria Pugliese

- Location: Via Giuseppe Parini, 14
- Phone: +39 0832 316857

Southern Italian cuisine spot, known for its flavorful Cavatelli pasta paired with various sauces.

- • - Tabisca "il Vico dei Tagliati"
- Location: Via Dietro Ospedale dei Pellegrini 29
- Phone: +39 380 634 4345

Quirky outdoor restaurant serving Pasticciotto, a baked pastry filled with custard cream.

- • - Mezzo Quinto
- Location: Via Degli Ammirati, 16
- Phone: +39 328 088 2474

Southern Italian eatery offering a variety of dishes, including Panzerotti and Focaccia Pugliese.

- • - 3 Rane
- Location: Via Cavour, 7
- Phone: +39 375 504 0165

Avant-garde cuisine in a rustic setting, featuring creative dishes like Gnummareddi fritters.

- • - La Cucina di Mamma Elvira
- Location: Via Ludovico Maremonti, 33
- Phone: +39 331 579 5127

Country-chic spot presenting homestyle meals, including the popular Puccia bread filled with various ingredients.

- • - Alle due Corti

- Location: Corte dei Giugni, 1, Via Leonardo Prato, 42
- Phone: +39 0832 242223

Cosy restaurant featuring Osteria 203, offering a menu with a variety of Italian dishes.

- • - Primo restaurant in lecce
- Location: Via 47 Reggimento Fanteria, 7
- Phone: +39 0832 243802

Fine dining experience showcasing Negroamaro Wine, a robust red wine variety from Puglia.

- • - A'Roma l'Osteria
- Location: Via Cesare Battisti, 3
- Phone: +39 366 247 4402

Roman osteria with a diverse menu, including Alle due Corti, offering a unique blend of Italian flavors.

- • - Osteria degli Spiriti
- Location: Via Cesare Battisti, 4
- Phone: +39 0832 246274

Italian osteria presenting Il Vico Del Gusto, a refined seafood restaurant with upscale surroundings.

Shopping

Below are recommendable shops in the city.
Explore shopping in any of these stores and bring back some souvenirs.

- - CENTRUM Centro commerciale
 - Type: Shopping mall
 - Address: Viale Giovanni Paolo II, 3
 A prominent shopping destination, CENTRUM Centro commerciale offers diverse in-store shopping experiences.

- - Spazio Centro Commerciale
 - Type: Shopping mall
 - Address: Via Vittorio Bachelet, 23
 Spazio Centro Commerciale, a bustling shopping hub, invites customers for a variety of in-store shopping options.

- - Lecce Food Market
 - Type: Shopping mall
 - Address: Via Adua
 - Phone: +39 351 020 1680
 Lecce Food Market, located on Via Adua, provides a unique space for in-store shopping experiences.

- - Spazio Outlet

- Type: Store
- Address: Piazza Mazzini Giuseppe, 31
- Phone: +39 0832 169 3134

Spazio Outlet offers in-store shopping along with kerbside pickup and delivery, providing a convenient shopping experience.

- • - Centro Commerciale Mongolfiera Lecce
- Type: Shopping mall
- Address: Surbo, Province of Lecce, Italy
- Phone: +39 0832 309205

Discover a wide range of shopping options at Centro Commerciale Mongolfiera Lecce, a popular shopping mall.

- • - Mercatino Porta rudiae
- Type: Shopping mall
- Address: Viale dell'Università, 99

Mercatino Porta rudiae, situated on Viale dell'Università, offers a unique in-store shopping experience.

- • - Mercato di Lecce
- Type: Shopping mall
- Address: Via Avellino, 10

Mercato di Lecce opens at 7 am on Mondays, providing a vibrant in-store shopping atmosphere.

- • - Francesca Carallo
- Type: Shopping mall
- Address: Vico dei Pensini, 1

- Phone: +39 328 948 2158
Francesca Carallo, a charming shopping spot at Vico Pensini, offers delightful in-store shopping.

- • - Artefare
- Type: Store
- Address: Via Arcivescovo Petronelli, 14
- Phone: +39 389 311 0222
Artefare, an inviting store on Via Arcivescovo Petronelli, caters to in-store shopping enthusiasts.

- • - Happy Shop
- Type: Store
- Address: Viale Francesco Lo Re
Happy Shop on Viale Francesco Lo Re provides an enjoyable in-store shopping experience until 9 pm.

- • - Calipso Store - LECCE
- Type: Boutique
- Address: Via Francesco Rubichi, 43
- Phone: +39 348 366 5280
Calipso Store - LECCE, a boutique on Via Francesco Rubichi, offers in-store shopping with kerbside pickup and delivery options.

- • - U.S. LECCE STORE by Salentinamente
- Type: Store
- Address: Via Fabio Filzi, 30
- Phone: +39 320 057 6481

U.S. LECCE STORE by Salentinamente welcomes shoppers for in-store shopping, in-store pick-up, and delivery services.

- - Fantasy Store Lecce
 - Type: Toy store
 - Address: Via Salvatore Trinchese, 13/A
 - Phone: +39 0832 665035
Fantasy Store Lecce, located on Via Salvatore Trinchese, provides a diverse selection of toys for in-store shopping.

- - Pinko Boutique Lecce
 - Type: Women's clothing store
 - Address: Via Salvatore Trinchese, 42/C
 - Phone: +39 0832 256031
   Pinko Boutique Lecce offers a range of women's clothing for in-store shopping and in-store pick-up.

- - Timberland Store
 - Type: Shoe store
 - Address: Via Vittorio Emanuele II, 39
 - Phone: +39 0832 302568
   Timberland Store, featuring stylish and rugged apparel, invites customers for in-store shopping until 8:30 pm.

- - Vico dei Bolognesi - Concept Store
 - Type: Women's clothing store
 - Address: Via Giacomo Matteotti, 22
 - Phone: +39 0832 301417

Vico Bolognesi - Concept Store offers a curated collection of women's clothing for in-store shopping, in-store pick-up, and delivery.

- • - Bershka
  - Type: Clothing store
  - Address: Via Salvatore Trinchese, 19
  - Phone: +39 0832 166 0150

Bershka, located on Via Salvatore Trinchese, welcomes shoppers for on-trend apparel and accessories in-store.

- • - ZARA
  - Type: Clothing store
  - Address: Via Salvatore Trinchese, 29
  - Phone: +39 02 3828 7157

ZARA, renowned for on-trend apparel and accessories, invites customers for in-store shopping until 8:30 pm.

- • - PJ Collection Lecce
  - Type: Fashion accessories store
  - Address: Via Templari, 18
  - Phone: +39 0832 241191

PJ Collection Lecce offers a diverse range of fashion accessories for in-store shopping, in-store pick-up, and delivery.

Phrases And Slang Terms

Basic Italian phrases and area slang terms to be familiar with before traveling.

- Buongiorno (Good morning)
- Buonasera (Good evening)
- Ciao (Hello/Goodbye)
- Grazie (Thank you)
- Prego (You're welcome)
- Per favore (Please)
- Mi scusì (Excuse me)
- Posso avere il conto? (Can I have the bill?)
- Dov'è il bagno? (Where is the bathroom?)
- costa? (How much does it cost?)
- Mi chiamo... (My name is...)
- Come ti ? (What is your name?)
- Parla inglese? (Do you speak English?)

- Mi aiuti, per favore? (Can you help me, please?)
- Vorrei... (I would like...)
- Posso scattare una foto? (Can I take a photo?)
- Dove si trova la stazione? (Where is the train station?)
- Dove posso trovare un ristorante? (Where can I find a restaurant?)
- Che ora è? (What time is it?)
- Vorrei prenotare un tavolo per due. (I would like to book a table for two.)
- Quanto tempo ci vuole per arrivare a...? (How long does it take to get to...?)

- Mi potrebbe consigliare un piatto tipico? (Could you recommend a local dish?)

- Che tipo di trasporto pubblico c'è a Lecce? (What kind of public transportation is there in Lecce?)

- Mi può consigliare un buon gelato? (Can you recommend a good gelato?)

- C'è una farmacia qui vicino? (Is there a pharmacy nearby?)

- Quale è la specialità culinaria di Lecce? (What is the culinary specialty of Lecce?)

- Posso pagare con carta di credito? (Can I pay with a credit card?)

- Mi potrebbe chiamare un taxi? (Could you call a taxi for me?)

- Dove posso comprare biglietti per le attrazioni turistiche? (Where can I buy tickets for tourist attractions?)

- Qual è la via principale di shopping a Lecce? (What is the main shopping street in Lecce?)

- Posso noleggiare una bicicletta qui? (Can I rent a bicycle here?)

- Ha una mappa della città? (Do you have a city map?)

- Posso avere un bicchiere d'acqua, per favore? (Can I have a glass of water, please?)

- Che tempo fa oggi? (What is the weather like today?)

- Mi potrebbe consigliare un buon ristorante di pesce? (Could you recommend a good seafood restaurant?)

- C'è un mercato tradizionale qui? (Is there a traditional market here?)

- Posso cambiare soldi qui? (Can I exchange money here?)
- Come si die in italiano...? (How do you say it in Italian...?)
- Mi potrebbe consigliare un bel posto per fare una passeggiata? (Could you recommend a nice place for a walk?)
- Cosa mi consiglia di visitare a Lecce? (What do you recommend I visit in Lecce?)

- Dove posso trovare un internet café? (Where can I find an internet café?)
- Quanto dista la spiaggia più vicina? (How far is the nearest beach?)
- Mi potrebbe consigliare un buon vino locale? (Could you recommend a good local wine?)
- Posso avere un menu in inglese? (Can I have a menu in English?)
- Quale è la specialità di caffè qui? (What is the local coffee specialty here?)
- Posso avere un adattatore elettrico? (Can I have an electrical adapter?)

- C'è un wifi gratuito qui? (Is there free Wifi here?)
- Mi potrebbe dire dov'è la stazione dei treni? (Could you tell me where the train station is?)
- Quanto costa un biglietto per il trasporto pubblico? (How much is a ticket for public transportation?)
- Ha un menu vegetariano? (Do you have a vegetarian menu?)

- Dove posso trovare un ufficio turistico? (Where can I find a tourist office?)
- Posso avere un depliant delle attrazioni turistiche? (Can I have a brochure of tourist attractions?)
- Qual è il modo migliore per raggiungere il centro città? (What is the best way to reach the city center?)

- C'è un orario di chiusura per i negozi? (Is there a closing time for shops?)
- Posso noleggiare un'auto qui? (Can I rent a car here?)
- Mi potrebbe consigliare una buona pasticceria? (Could you recommend a good pastry shop?)
- Quale è il ristorante più famoso di Lecce? (What is the most famous restaurant in Lecce?)
- Posso avere il tuo numero di telefono? (Can I have your phone number?)

- C'è un supermercato qui vicino? (Is there a supermarket nearby?)
- Qual è il miglior periodo dell'anno per visitare Lecce? (What is the best time of year to visit Lecce?)
- Posso prenotare un tour della città qui? (Can I book a city tour here?)
- Quanto costa un taxi da qui all'aeroporto? (How much is a taxi from here to the airport?)
- C'è un servizio di consegna cibo qui? (Is there a food delivery service here?)
- Mi potrebbe consigliare una buona gelateria artigianale? (Could you recommend a good artisanal ice cream shop?)

- Posso pagare con carta di debito? (Can I pay with a debit card?)
- Quanto dura il viaggio in treno da Lecce a...? (How long is the train journey from Lecce to...?)
- Posso avere il menu del giorno? (Can I have the daily menu?)

- Dove posso trovare un buon caffè? (Where can I find good coffee?)
- Quanto costa una corsa in taxi qui? (How much does a taxi ride cost here?)
- Mi potrebbe dire dove posso trovare un bancomat? (Could you tell me where I can find an ATM?)
- C'è un parcheggio qui vicino? (Is there parking nearby?)
- Posso avere un cuscino extra, per favore? (Can I have an extra pillow, please?)
- Ha una mappa turistica della città? (Do you have a tourist map of the city?)
- Quale è il miglior ristorante di cucina tradizionale a Lecce? (What is the best traditional cuisine restaurant in Lecce?)
- Posso avere un tavolo con vista? (Can I have a table with a view?)

- C'è una tassa di soggiorno qui? (Is there a tourist tax here?)
- Mi potrebbe consigliare una buona enoteca? (Could you recommend a good wine bar?)
- Quanto dista la

stazione ferroviaria da qui? (How far is the train station from here?)

- Posso avere il tuo indirizzo email? (Can I have your email address?)

- Ha un servizio di lavanderia qui? (Do you have a laundry service here?)

- Quale è la chiesa più antica di Lecce? (What is the oldest church in Lecce?)

- Posso pagare in contanti? (Can I pay in cash?)

- Qual è il tuo piatto preferito della cucina locale? (What is your favorite dish from local cuisine?)

- C'è una zona wifi gratuita qui? (Is there a free Wi-Fi zone here?)

- Mi potrebbe consigliare un buon agriturismo nei dintorni? (Could you recommend a good farmhouse stay in the surroundings?)

- Quale è il museo più interessante di Lecce? (What is the most interesting museum in Lecce?)

- Posso avere un secchio di ghiaccio in camera? (Can I have a bucket of ice in my room?)

- Ha uno sconto per studenti? (Do you have a student discount?)

- Quanto costa un biglietto per l'ingresso al castello? (How much is a ticket for the castle entrance?)

- Posso avere un asciugacapelli in camera? (Can I have a hairdryer in my room?)

- Che tipo di vino consiglia con questo piatto? (What type of wine do you recommend with this dish?)

- Posso avere una coperta extra, per favore? (Can I have an extra blanket, please?)

- Benvenuto a Lecce! Spero che il tuo soggiorno sia piacevole. (Welcome to Lecce! I hope your stay is enjoyable.)
- Se hai domande o hai bisogno di informazioni aggiuntive, non esitare a chiedere alla reception. (If you have any questions or need additional information, feel free to ask at the reception.)

- Lecce è famosa per la sua architettura barocca. Ti consiglio di esplorare il centro storico per ammirare le bellezze della città. (Lecce is famous for its Baroque architecture. I recommend exploring the historic center to admire the city's beauties.)
- Assicurati di assaporare la cucina locale, ricca di sapori autentici. I piatti a base di pesce e i formaggi tipici sono imperdibili. (Make sure to savor the local cuisine, rich in authentic flavors. Seafood dishes and typical cheeses are a must-try.)

- Lecce è conosciuta anche per la sua vita notturna vibrante. Scopri i locali e i bar della città per vivere appieno l'atmosfera serale. (Lecce is also known for its vibrant nightlife. Explore the city's clubs and bars to fully experience the evening atmosphere.)
- Se vuoi fare un'escursione fuori città, la costa salentina offre spiagge incantevoli. Chiedi alla reception informazioni su escursioni o noleggio auto. (If you want to take a trip outside the city, the Salento coast offers

enchanting beaches. Ask the reception for information on excursions or car rentals.)

- Durante il tuo soggiorno, assicurati di visitare la Basilica di Santa Croce, un capolavoro dell'architettura barocca leccese. (During your stay, make sure to visit the Basilica of Santa Croce, a masterpiece of Lecce's Baroque architecture.)

- Per un'esperienza autentica, prova a parlare qualche parola in italiano con i locali. Saranno felici di vedere il tuo interesse per la cultura locale. (For an authentic experience, try speaking a few words in Italian with the locals. They will be happy to see your interest in the local culture.)

- Nel caso in cui avessi bisogno di assistenza medica, chiedi alla reception o cerca il numero di emergenza locale. (In case you need medical assistance, ask at the reception or look for the local emergency number.)

- Quando visiti i monumenti, rispetta le regole e la storia del luogo. Lecce è ricca di storia e cultura, e il rispetto contribuisce a preservarla. (When visiting monuments, respect the rules and history of the place. Lecce is rich in history and culture, and your respect contributes to its preservation.)

- Se vuoi esplorare la campagna circostante, considera un'escursione in bicicletta. Chiedi alla reception informazioni sul noleggio biciclette e sui percorsi consigliati. (If you want to explore the surrounding countryside, consider a cycling excursion. Ask at the reception for information on bike rentals and recommended routes.)

- Assicurati di avere una bottiglia d'acqua con te mentre esplori la città, specialmente durante le giornate calde. (Make sure to have a water bottle with you while exploring the city, especially on hot days.)

- Ricorda di confermare gli orari di apertura e chiusura delle attrazioni turistiche prima di visitarle per evitare sorprese. (Remember to confirm the opening and closing hours of tourist attractions before visiting to avoid surprises.)
- Lecce è conosciuta per le sue ceramiche artigianali. Se cerchi souvenir autentici, visita le botteghe artigiane nel centro storico. (Lecce is known for its artisanal ceramics. If you're looking for authentic souvenirs, visit the craft shops in the historic center.)

- Se hai bisogno di indicazioni stradali, chiedi ai passanti o usa app di mappe per orientarsi facilmente. (If you need directions, ask locals or use map apps to navigate easily.)- Per una colazione tipica, cerca un bar locale che serva cornetti e caffè. È un ottimo modo per iniziare la giornata come un vero italiano. (For a typical breakfast, look for a local bar serving croissants and coffee. It's a great way to start the day like a true Italian.)

- Se vuoi fare uno spuntino veloce, cerca una panineria locale e assapora un panino con prosciutto e formaggio. (If you want a quick snack, look for a local sandwich shop and enjoy a sandwich with ham and cheese.)

- Sii consapevole dell'orario della "siesta". In molti negozi e ristoranti, potresti trovare chiuso nel pomeriggio. (Be aware of the "siesta" time. In many shops and restaurants, you might find them closed in the afternoon.)
- Assicurati di avere una piccola quantità di contanti con te, specialmente in luoghi più tradizionali che potrebbero non accettare carte di credito. (Make sure to have a small amount of cash with you, especially in more traditional places that may not accept credit cards.)

Slang Terms
- Baretto - Small local bar or pub.
- Scialla - Relax or chill out, often used to convey a laid-back attitude.
- Chiù - More, used to express a desire for more of something.
- Fico - Cool or awesome.
- Mica male - Not bad, used to describe something that is pretty good.
- Pischello - Youngster or newbie.

- Stare al fresco - Hanging out or spending time outdoors.
- Accussì - Like this or in this way.
- Bravo - Well done or good job.
- Allucinante - Mind-blowing or amazing.
- Fai il salentino - Act like a local from Salento.
- Pupi - Guys or friends.
- Magari - Maybe or I wish.
- Fregarsene - To not care about something.

- In gamba - Skilled or talented.
- Facciamo tardi - Let's stay out late.
- Burlone - Jokester or prankster.
- Spaccare - To rock or excel at something.
- Basta cosi - That's enough or stop it.
- Cazzeggio - Wasting time or goofing off.
- Sbragare - To show off or boast.

- A chitarra - Playing the guitar, often associated with impromptu music sessions.
- Fatti i fatti tuoi - Mind your own business.
- Gnamo - Let's go, hurry up.
- Figo - Stylish or fashionable.
- Ammucchiata - A group gathering or a crowded place.
- Aranzeta - A loud argument or commotion.
- Accattà - To buy or purchase.
- Sciummo - Money.
- Leverare - To leave or go away.
- Cavare gli occhi - To be amazed or impressed.
- Pulcino - A cute girl or young woman.
- Ehila' - Hey there or hello.

- Stai de volo - Mind your own business.
- Quaglia - Easy or simple.
- Mastro - Skilled or experienced person.
- Che palle! - What a bore! or How boring!
- Vattelapesca - Go figure or who knows.
- Ahi, ahi - Ouch or that hurts.
- Chiù puglia ca salentu - More Puglia than Salento, implying someone is acting more from the northern region of Puglia.

- Ballo - Party or dance.
- Malandrino - Mischievous person.
- Girone - A group of friends.
- Magheggia - To figure something out or find a solution.
- Essere in giro - To be around or out and about.
- Uè - Hey or yo.
- Tacatà - A mix of dancing and moving energetically.
- Andare a mazzi - To go in a group or together.
- Stai fresco - Forget it or no way.

Fat Facts (Puglia)

Puglia is difficult to describe in a single word because of its diverse range of regions, ecosystems, and life rhythms. Le Puglie, which translates to "many Puglia" in Italian, is a term used by certain older Italians to describe the southern Italian region of Puglia. Although Le Puglie no longer exists, you'll understand why when you visit.

The "boot heel" of Italy is outlined by Puglia's 940 km (584 mi) of coastline, which was formerly a part of the Magna Graecia and was home to the powerful flotillas of the ancient Romans. A few locations have garnered media attention in the last ten years due to their extravagant weddings and use as summer getaways by famous people.

Best time to visit Puglia

When most Italians take their mandatory summer holidays in July and August, Puglia is busy: hotels are expensive and book up months in advance, beaches are packed, and the weather can turn extremely hot, with some days reaching temperatures beyond 42°C (106°F).

The nightlife flourishes during this period. Music events like Locus and Notte della Taranta attract musicians from all over the world, clubs in the Salento region play music nonstop until dawn, and town squares come alive to celebrate sagre di paese, the much anticipated annual religious and culinary fairs.

The region's warm temperature provides 25°C (77°F) days as early as April and into October, making it the perfect location if you're searching for serenity, quaint towns, and empty crystal-clear lakes.

The region's pleasant climate occurs before and after the two core summer months. It's also a great time to explore the verdant countryside and sample some of the local olive oil and wine. Without the burden of the peak season, hotels become more reasonably priced and the standard of the food and services improves.

From November to March, you may find yourself travelling alone. Throughout the season, a few hotels and eateries close, and public services are reduced. Nevertheless, it might be the ideal moment to grab an espresso at a local café and strike up a conversation with a pugliese.

Many will take the time to tell you which local eatery is their favourite and why their town's panzerotto (fried pastry), tiedda (Bari's famous rice potatoes and mussels dish), or grape variety is, hands down, the best.

How to travel to and within Puglia

The primary entry points to the area are the two major airports at Bari and Brindisi. Reasonably frequent high-speed trains arrive in Puglia from Rome, Naples, and Milan. Ferry boats connect Bari and Brindisi to Albania, Greece, and Croatia. But to be honest, once you're in Puglia, you might want to rent a car if you want to really enjoy the region.

Renting a car will enable you to see several locations on the same day, even if you are only here for a weekend, and avoid using the frequently problematic public transportation system.

Numerous tour companies arrange group bicycle excursions across the area. It's typical to come across groups of explorers cycling along the route in the less heated months of spring and autumn.

My preferred activity in Puglia
Spend a day travelling the coastal route in Salento that links Otranto and Santa Maria di Leuca. While travelling, make a swim stop at one of the rocky bays with access to the sea, such as Grotta Zinzulusa in Castro. Next, enjoy a sweet pasticciotto at Martinucci paired with a caffè leccese, an espresso shot served with ice and a finger of almond syrup.

Continue driving until you get to Tricase Porto, where you may take another dip in the crystal-clear port waters. Climb the stairs to Caffe d'Oltremare to cap off the day with a glass of Negroamaro wine, some taralli, and pickled olives. Enjoy the azure Mediterranean as you relax on the open terrace with a view of the ocean. It will feel good to slow down and enjoy the moment.

In Puglia, how much money will I need?

As far as travel to Italy goes, Puglia offers generally fair value. You get excellent cuisine and drinks at reasonable pricing. Puglia is referred to as "the garden of Italy" since so many fruits and vegetables are grown there, and this can be tasted in the flavours of the food. Two €2 coins can be used to pay for coffee, and two more for a sandwich.

However, keep an eye out in July and August in more well-known locations like Gallipoli or Polignano a Mare, since prices for Peroni beers might unexpectedly increase from €3 to three times their off-season value.

An estimated daily cost for a room at the Puglia hostel is €60.
Standard room for two: from €100 to €120

Apartment for self-catering (including Airbnb): from €140 A single journey on public transport costs €2, and a day pass costs €3.50.

Panzerotti: €2, coffee: €2, and a sandwich from a bakery: €4.
€80 for a bottle of local wine and dinner for two.
Pint of beer at the bar: €3.

Printed in Great Britain
by Amazon

42894979R00056